Friends Forever, Snoopy

 LITTLE SIMON
An imprint of Simon & Schuster Children's Publishing Division
1230 Avenue of the Americas
New York, New York 10020

Manufactured in the United States of America
First Edition
10 9 8 7 6 5 4 3 2 1
Library of Congress Cataloging-in-Publication Data
Boczkowski, Tricia
  Friends forever, Snoopy / based on the comic strips by Charles M. Schulz ; adapted by Tricia Boczkowski.—1st ed.
    p. cm. — (Ready-to-read)
  "Peanuts"
 Summary: Celebrates the friendship enjoyed by Snoopy, Charlie Brown, and the whole Peanuts gang.
  ISBN 0-689-84597-9 (alk. Paper)
  [1. Friendship—Fiction. 2. Beagle (Dog breed)—Fiction. 3. Dogs—Fiction.] I. Schulz, Charles M. II. Title. III. Series.

PZ7.B63355 Fr 2001
[E]-dc21   2001035825

Friends Forever, Snoopy

Based on the comic strips
by Charles M. Schulz
Adapted by Patricia Boczkowski
Art adapted by Nick and Peter LoBianco

Ready-to-Read

LITTLE SIMON

New York   London   Toronto   Sydney   Singapore

**Come rain or come shine,
friends are always there
when you need them.**

One night Snoopy was
sleeping on top of his doghouse.
It started to rain.
Good grief, he thought,
opening his eyes.

I'm drowning!
Snoopy sat up.
Where are all my friends? he shouted.

Woodstock and his friends
came with umbrellas.
They held the umbrellas
over Snoopy.
He went back to sleep
and stayed nice and dry.
It's nice to have friends!

Friends stick together.

Snoopy is a good friend
to the birds, too.

One summer day Lucy said to Snoopy,
"I don't mind sharing my pool with you on a
hot day."

So Snoopy invited his bird friends
in for a swim.
Lucy was not happy.
"This is ridiculous!" she cried.
But the birds had already put on their snorkel
masks.

Everybody stayed nice and cool.

Friends always take care of one another.

One day Snoopy was telling Woodstock about a holiday.

"They work for days ahead of time," Snoopy said. "And on Thanksgiving Day they roast this bird . . ."

Woodstock's eyes grew wide with fear.

11

KLUNK!

Woodstock fell off Snoopy's doghouse.

Snoopy scooped Woodstock up
and hugged him tight.

"Oh, little friend of friends,
don't worry," said Snoopy.

He hugged Woodstock closer.

"No one is going to roast *you!*"

"If anyone tried to roast you for Thanksgiving dinner," Snoopy said, "you know what I'd do?"

Just then Charlie Brown stopped by.
"I'd punch him in the nose!!"
exclaimed Snoopy.

BONK!

Woodstock was comforted.

He knew that Snoopy would never
let anything bad happen to him.

He stretched out on Snoopy's belly
and they both fell fast asleep.

Friends always stick up for one another.

One day Snoopy and the gang were
waiting in line for movie tickets.

Dogs were not allowed in the movie theater.

The ticket salesman was giving Snoopy a
hard time.

But his friends stuck by him.

"Go ahead! Let him in!" yelled Lucy.

"Show a little kindness!" Linus chimed in.

"Let him in!" demanded Peppermint Patty.

"Show a little love!" pleaded Marcy.

"Let him in!" shouted Franklin.

"Show a little compassion!" ordered Violet.

Snoopy looked at the ticket salesman proudly and thought, These are my friends.

Sometimes friends disappoint you.

Snoopy was very excited.

Woodstock had invited him
to play hockey with the birds.

When he got to the birdbath,
Snoopy waited to get in the game.
    It was a while before he realized that
Woodstock didn't want him
to actually play hockey . . .

All they wanted me to do
was drive the Zamboni,
he realized sadly.

Friends share.

Charlie Brown and Snoopy
were sitting under a tree.
"Here we are," said Charlie Brown.
He fed Snoopy half of his sandwich.
"We're two old friends
sharing a sandwich."

Charlie Brown was happy.

"It doesn't get any better than this!" he said.

Snoopy's mouth was full.

It doesn't get any better than *this?* he wondered.

Then he realized that sharing with friends *is* better than most things!

Friends help one another.

Lucy looked out her back door.
"It snowed again last night,"
she said.

Woodstock was up to his
neck in the snow.

"Those birds look hungry,"
Lucy said to Linus.

"I am making bread crumbs for the birds,"
Linus said.

"You should bring napkins, too,"
said Lucy.

Friends understand one another.

Charlie Brown and Snoopy were sitting under a tree.

"You don't have to worry, Snoopy," said Charlie Brown.

"I'd never sell you. You and I are friends. We're buddies.

In fact, you're the best thing that's ever happened to me."

"I know," said Snoopy, who was ready for a nap.

Snoopy and Charlie Brown are friends forever.